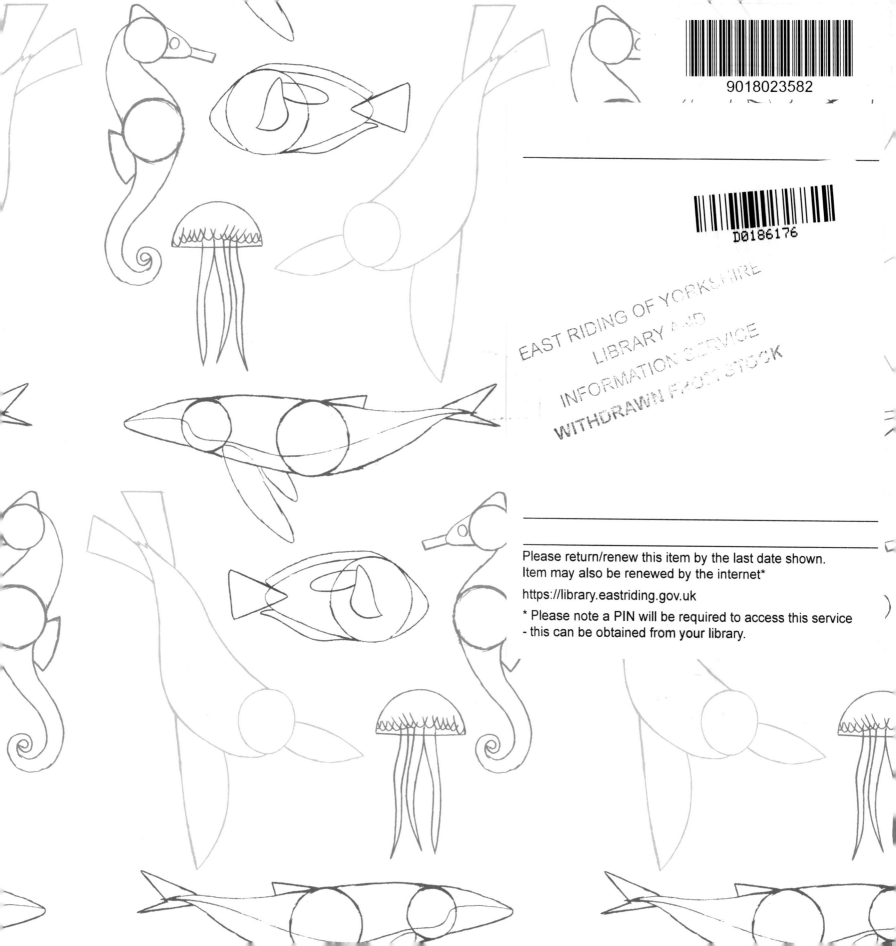

This book belongs to:

•••

•••

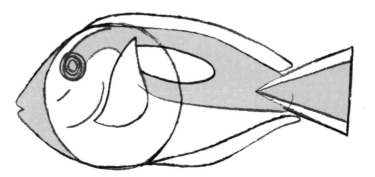

GRAFFEG

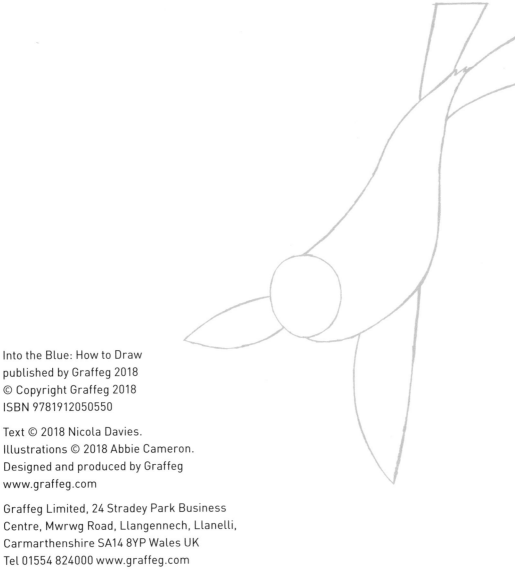

Into the Blue: How to Draw
published by Graffeg 2018
© Copyright Graffeg 2018
ISBN 9781912050550

Text © 2018 Nicola Davies.
Illustrations © 2018 Abbie Cameron.
Designed and produced by Graffeg
www.graffeg.com

Graffeg Limited, 24 Stradey Park Business
Centre, Mwrwg Road, Llangennech, Llanelli,
Carmarthenshire SA14 8YP Wales UK
Tel 01554 824000 www.graffeg.com

The publisher gratefully acknowledges the
financial support of this book by the Welsh
Books Council www.gwales.com

INTO THE BLUE

How to Draw

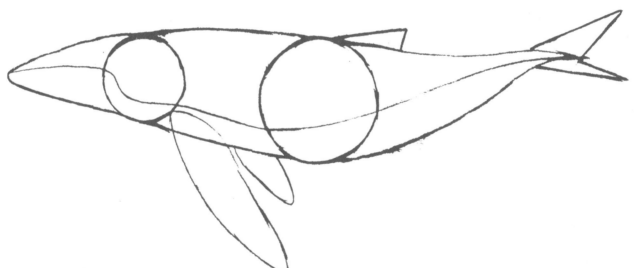

Written by
NicolaDavies

Illustrated by
AbbieCameron

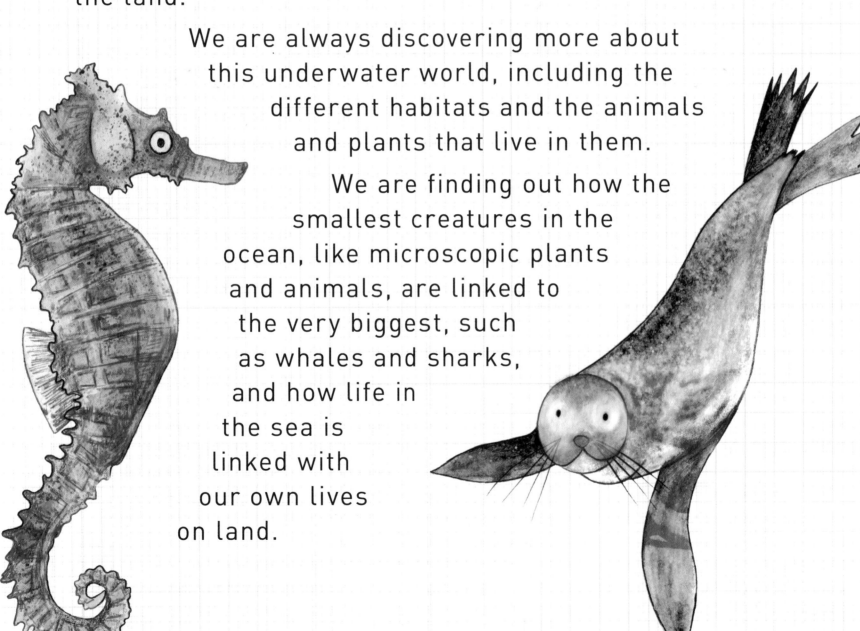

Almost three quarters of our planet is covered by the sea and creatures live in every part of it, from the sunlit surface to the very deepest, darkest depths.

Altogether, the sea offers far more living space than the land.

We are always discovering more about this underwater world, including the different habitats and the animals and plants that live in them.

We are finding out how the smallest creatures in the ocean, like microscopic plants and animals, are linked to the very biggest, such as whales and sharks, and how life in the sea is linked with our own lives on land.

There is so much to discover!
One of the most exciting jobs
in the world is to be a scientist
studying living things in
the ocean.

Learn to draw some of the
most amazing animals you can
find in the ocean by following
the step-by-step instructions
in this book.

Here are some drawing materials you can use:

✓
- ☐ Drawing pad
- ☐ Felt pens
- ☐ Colour pencils
- ☐ Crayons
- ☐ Drawing pencil
- ☐ Rubber
- ☐ Sharpener

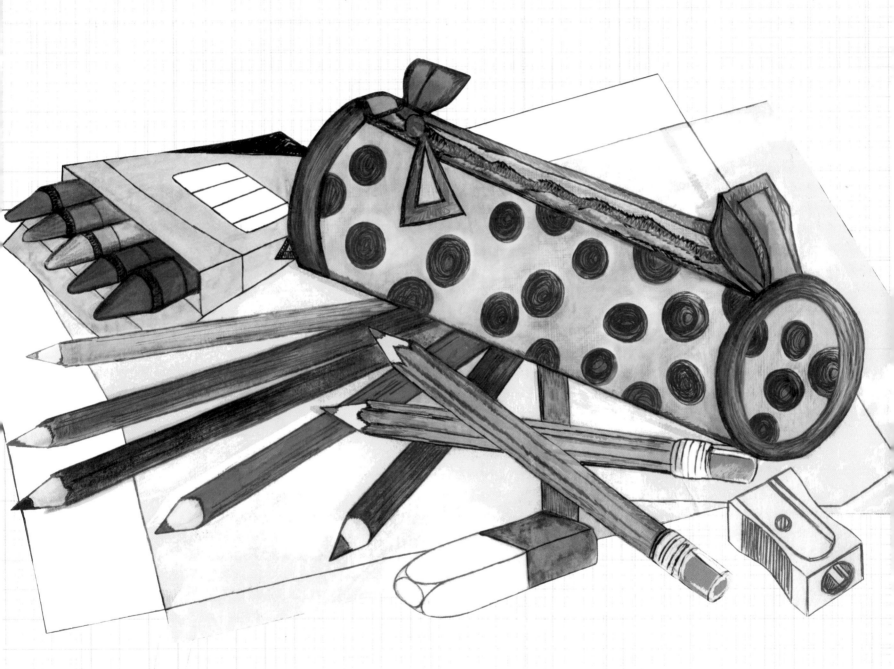

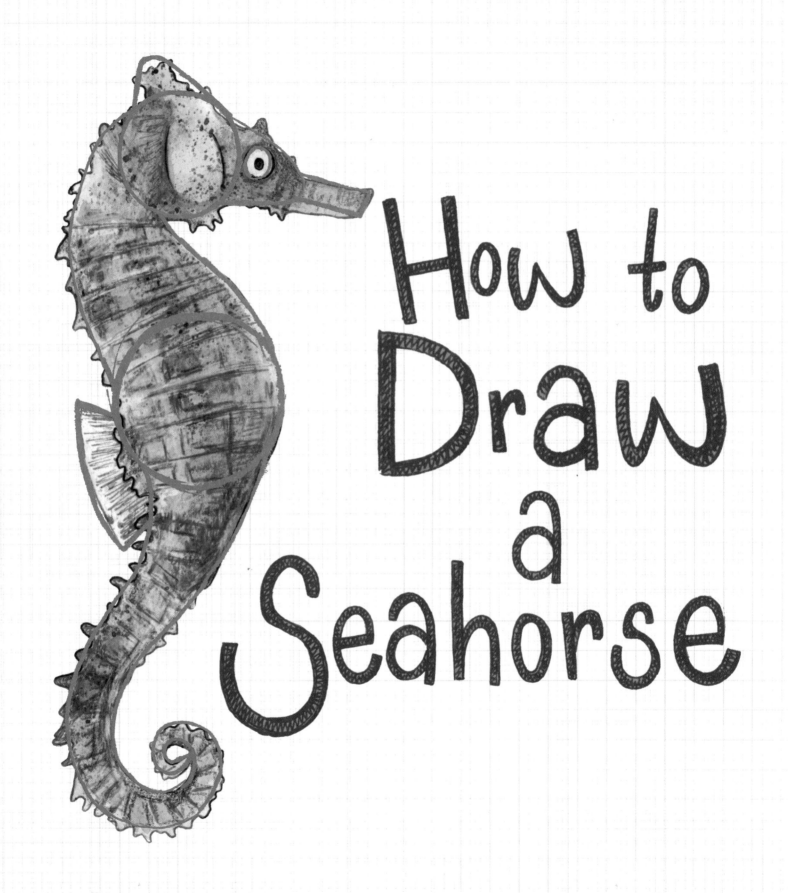

How to Draw a Seahorse

Step 1

Draw a circle.

Step 2

Place a smaller circle above it.

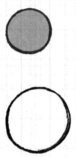

Step 3

Add a curved shape followed by a rectangular shape to form the head.

Step 4

Draw a line which loops around on itself as an outline for the tail.

Step 5

Connect both parts of your drawing and make a second looping line to complete the tail.

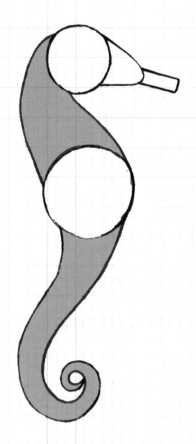

Step 6

Draw in the shape of the fin and the top of the head. Add a small eye to the face.

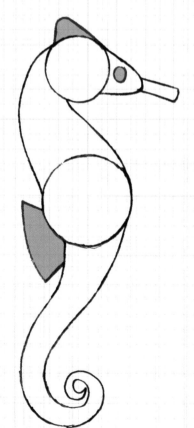

Step 7

Add details to the seahorse's body.

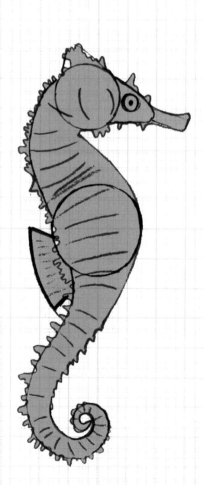

Step 8

Add colour to your drawing and make the scales really stand out with some shading.

Did you Know?

There are seahorses smaller than your little finger and some bigger than your hand. Most live in tropical waters but there are some off the UK coast. These strange fish have an unusual trait; the males are the ones who get pregnant. The females put their eggs into a pouch on the front of the male's body. Inside, little sea foals grow, and when they are ready the male gives birth to them and cares for them for the early part of their lives.

How to Draw a Humpback Whale

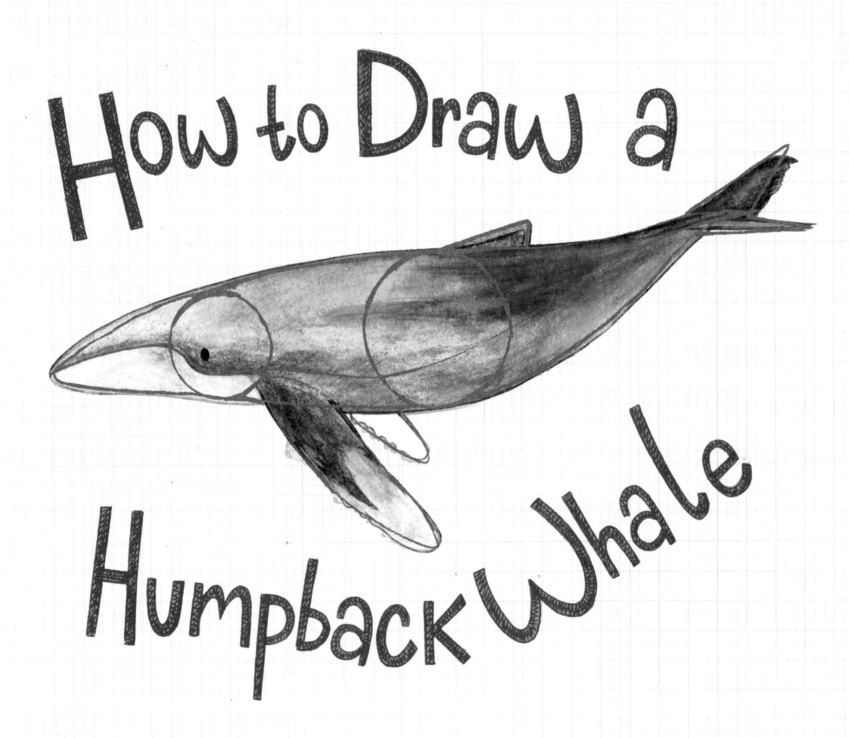

Step 1

Draw a circle.

Step 2

Place a smaller circle to the right and slightly below the first.

Step 3

Draw two triangular 'tails' coming away from the circles.

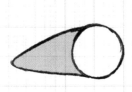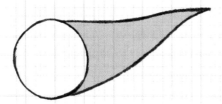

Step 4

Connect up both sections and draw a curved line running through the middle of them to complete the body.

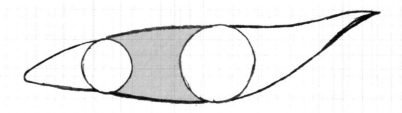

Step 5

Draw two curved shapes coming out from the body and add triangular shapes on top for the fins and at the end for the tail.

Step 6

Fill in the tail, the eye and some detail on the belly with a number of straight lines.

Step 7

Colour the whale and add some shading around the belly, fins and tail.

Did you Know?

Humpback whales travel from their feeding grounds in the polar seas (north or south poles) to the tropics and back every year. In warm, tropical waters they do their courtship and give birth to their young. During this process the male humpbacks sing incredible, long, complicated songs, composed of repeated phrases of whoops, rumbles, whistles and howls. It doesn't sound attractive and yet it is; humpback song is beautiful and the most complex display made by any non-human animal. But here is the really mind-blowing bit: all the male humpbacks in one location sing the same song as each other, but the following year the song will have changed. Over time, the song gradually evolves, as if all the males decide on adding a new verse or a different melody each year.

How to Draw a Blue Tang

Step 1

Draw a circle.

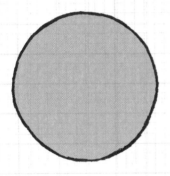

Step 2

Draw a curved shape out from the circle.

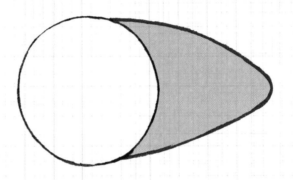

Step 3

Add a smaller curved shape to the opposite side.

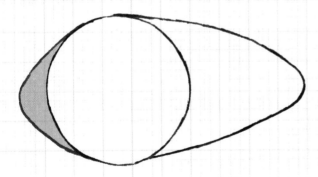

Step 4

Draw a triangle shape for the tail.

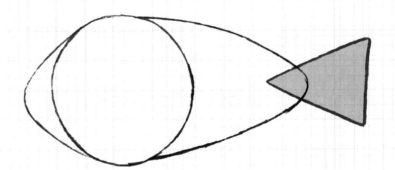

Step 5

Draw in two curved lines on the top and bottom of the fish's body.

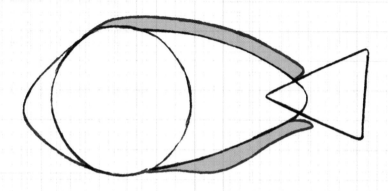

Step 6

Draw the fish's fin and an oval marking on it's side.

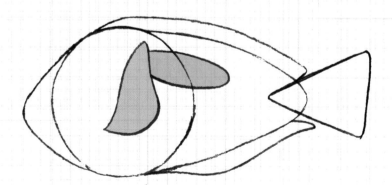

Step 7

Place several circles inside one another to make the eye, and add a few lines of detail to the body.

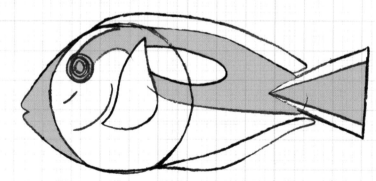

Step 8

Blue tang fish are highly recognisable because of their striking blue, yellow and black colour scheme, which you can add to your drawing.

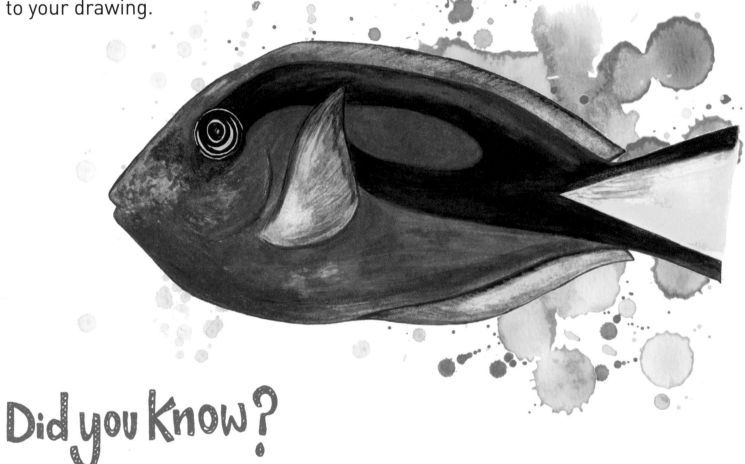

Did you know?

Thanks to Dory from the movie *Finding Dory*, everyone knows that blue tangs live on coral reefs. They live in pairs or small groups, a bit like Dory and her mum and dad do, but they don't take care of their young. In fact, they just lay their eggs in the water and the baby fish that hatch from them have to take care of themselves. They have an important role to play in coral reefs as they graze on seaweed, stopping it from growing all over the coral and suffocating it.

How to Draw a Seal

Step 1

Draw a circle.

Step 2

Draw a a curved, pointy shape extending up from the circle.

Step 3

Add two pointed fins, one from the head and one from the body.

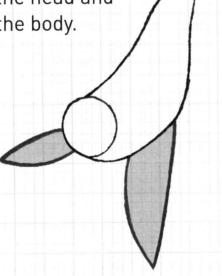

Step 4

For the tail, draw two fan shapes at the end of the body.

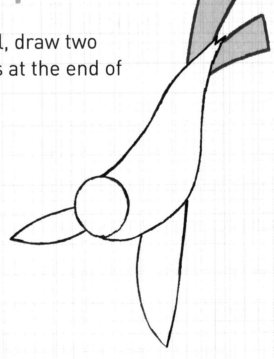

Step 5

Connect both halves together using curved lines.

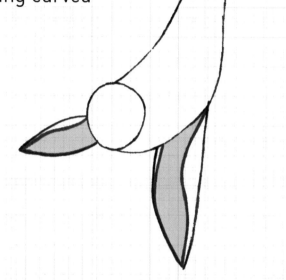

Step 6

Draw in the shape of the seal's flippers and feet.

Step 7

Add some details to the drawing with the eye, ear, nose and whiskers.

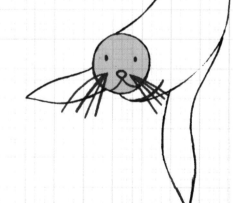

Step 8

Colour the seal grey and add some definition in black around the body and flippers.

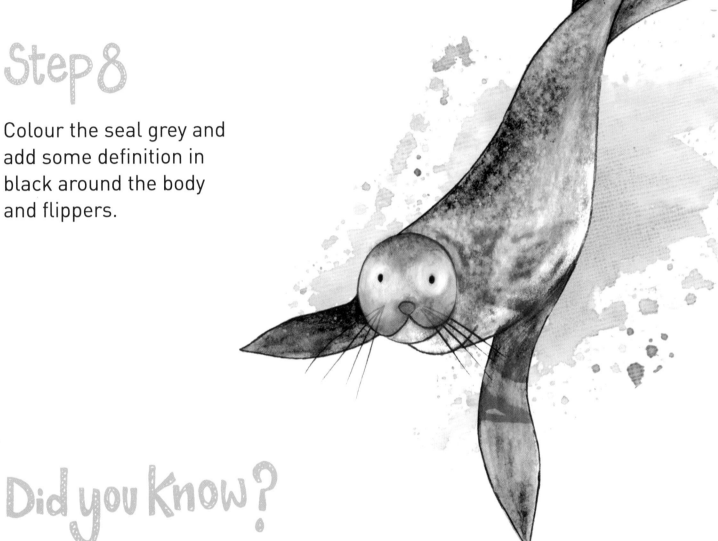

Did you know?

Grey seals live in cool north Atlantic waters round the coasts of Europe, Canada and the USA. They have long, straight noses, which makes them easy to tell apart from common seals. They can dive down as deep as 70 metres, finding fish with their sensitive whiskers and big eyes, which work well in low light. At low tide they often lie on rocks to dry their fur, sunbathe and rest.

How to
Draw
a
Jelly-
fish

Step 1

Draw a semicircle for the jellyfish's body.

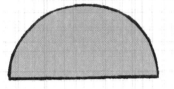

Step 2

Add some markings to the body.

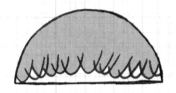

Step 3

Draw three long curving lines down from the body and connect them at the bottom.

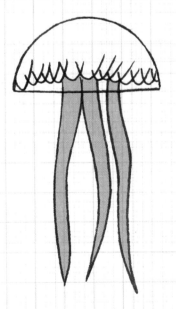

Step 4

Begin adding detail to the tentacles with rough lines.

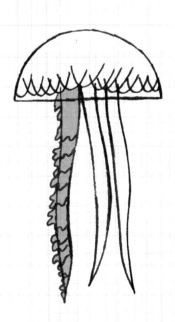

Step 5

Continue making rough lines along each of the tentacles to give them texture.

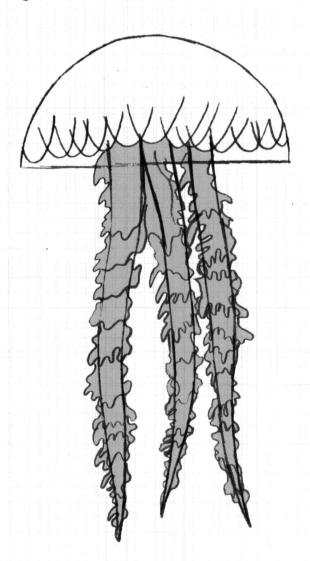

Step 6

Draw a final few lines out from the body, and put in some shading at the bottom of the body.

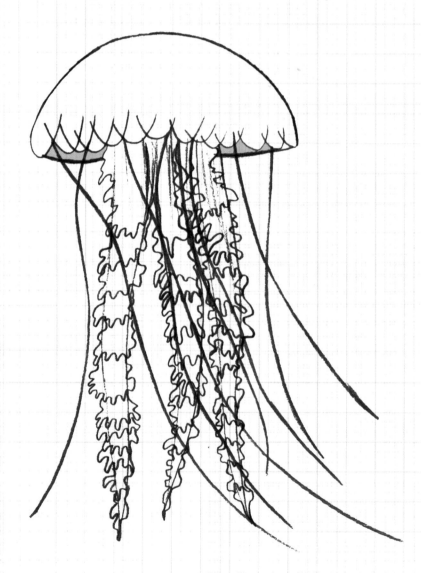

Step 7

Lightly colour your jellyfish in pink to give it a see-through effect.

Did you know?

Jellyfish are some of the simplest and oldest forms of life on earth. Their bell shaped bodies pulse gently, not strongly enough to swim against a current but just enough to keep them from sinking. Their long tentacles are covered with thousands of stinging cells, like tiny harpoons, that fire on contact with tiny creatures in the water. The tentacles feed what they have caught to the mouth in the centre of the bell.

Nicola Davies

Nicola is an award-winning author, whose many books for children include *The Promise* (Green Earth Book Award 2015, CILIP Kate Greenaway Shortlist 2015), *Tiny* (AAAS Subaru Prize 2015), *A First Book of Nature*, *Whale Boy* (Blue Peter Award Shortlist 2014), and the *Heroes of the Wild* series (Portsmouth Book Prize 2014). Nicola graduated in Zoology, studied whales and bats and then worked for the BBC Natural History Unit. Underlying all Nicola's writing is the belief that a relationship with nature is essential to every human being, and that now, more than ever, we need to renew that relationship. Nicola's children's books from Graffeg include *The Pond*, *Perfect* (CILIP Kate Greenaway Longlist 2017), the *Shadows and Light* series, *Animal Surprises*, *The Word Bird* and *Into the Blue*.

Abbie Cameron

Abbie Cameron was raised on the farmlands of the West Country. Surrounded by nature, she developed a love and appreciation for all creatures great and small. Abbie studied Illustration at University of Wales Trinity Saint David, where she first met Nicola Davies. Her style is playful and inventive, sharing some of the tongue-in-cheek attitude and doodle-like style of other contemporary British illustrators. Abbie employs the use of bright colours and texture, whilst playing with scale, composition and open space. Her other books include *Animal Surprises* (The Klaus Flugge Prize for the Most Exciting Newcomer to Picture Book Illustration Longlist 2017), *The Word Bird* and *Into the Blue*. Abbie was also highly commended for the Penguin Random House Design Awards 2014.

Rhyming Book Series

Discover the delights of nature with zoologist and top children's author Nicola Davies. Follow the young adventurer as she treks through the jungle in *Animal Surprises*, dives deep down into the sea in *Into the Blue* and climbs up high into the trees in *The Word Bird*. All three rhyming books are fully illustrated in colour by Abbie Cameron.

Titles in the series:
- **Animal Surprises**
- **The Word Bird**
- **Into the Blue**
- **The Secret of the Egg**
- **Invertebrates are Cool**
- **The Versatile Reptile**

How to Draw Series

In these step-by-step how to draw books, Abbie Cameron teaches children how to draw their favourite animals from the rhyming book series, alongside informative text from Nicola Davies about each species.

Titles in the series:
- **Animal Surprises: How to Draw**
- **The Word Bird: How to Draw**
- **Into the Blue: How to Draw**

Visit **www.graffeg.com/howtodraw** to watch Abbie drawing some of the animals from the series with step-by-step instructions.

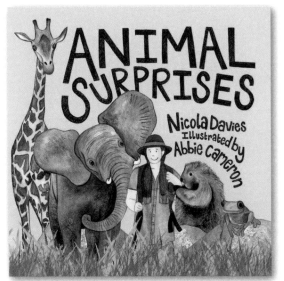

Animal Surprises

ISBN 9781910862445

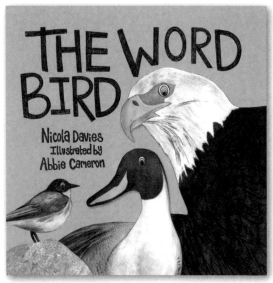

The Word Bird

ISBN 9781910862438

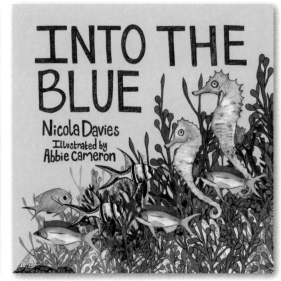

Into the Blue

ISBN 9781910862452

Animal Surprises: How to Draw

ISBN 9781912050567

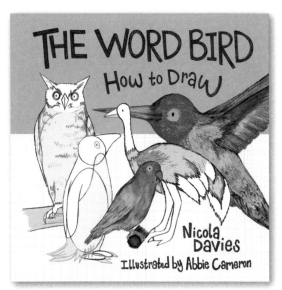

The Word Bird: How to Draw

ISBN 9781912050574

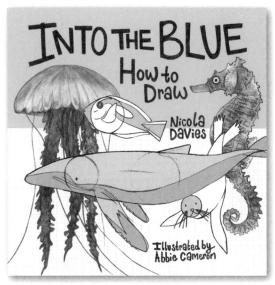

Into the Blue: How to Draw

ISBN 9781912050550

GRAFFEG

www.graffeg.com

Drawing Pages